SOBRIETY
and
Addiction Recovery
Journal
COLORING BOOK

BELONGS TO

_____

_____

Everyday
is a fresh
Start

NEVER LOSE HOPE

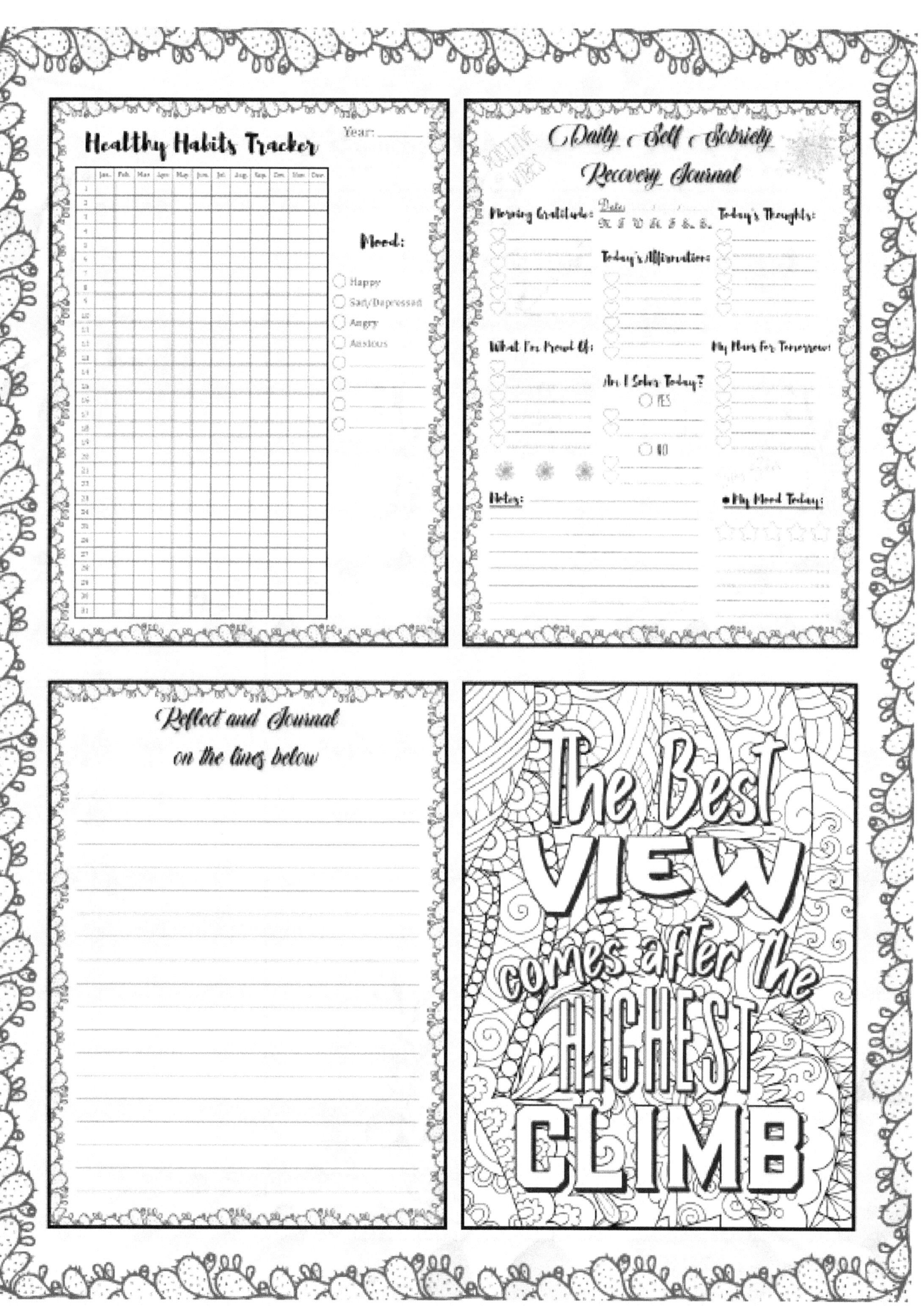

Healthy Habits Tracker

Year: _____

	Jan.	Feb.	Mar.	Apr.	May	Jun.	Jul.	Aug.	Sep.	Oct.	Nov.	Dec.
1												
2												
3												
4												
5												
6												
7												
8												
9												
10												
11												
12												
13												
14												
15												
16												
17												
18												
19												
20												
21												
22												
23												
24												
25												
26												
27												
28												
29												
30												
31												

Mood:

○ Happy
○ Sad/Depressed
○ Angry
○ Anxious
○
○
○

Daily Self Sobriety Recovery Journal

YOU'RE VIBES

Morning Gratitude: Date: ____
M T W Th F S S.

Today's Affirmations

Today's Thoughts:

What I'm Proud Of:

Am I Sober Today?
○ YES
○ NO

My Plans For Tomorrow:

Notes:

♦ My Mood Today:

Reflect and Journal
on the lines below

The Best VIEW comes after the HIGHEST CLIMB

Healthy Habits Tracker

Year: _____

	Jan.	Feb.	Mar.	Apr.	May.	Jun.	Jul.	Aug.	Sep.	Oct.	Nov.	Dec.
1												
2												
3												
4												
5												
6												
7												
8												
9												
10												
11												
12												
13												
14												
15												
16												
17												
18												
19												
20												
21												
22												
23												
24												
25												
26												
27												
28												
29												
30												
31												

Mood:

◯ Happy

◯ Sad/Depressed

◯ Angry

◯ Anxious

◯ _____

◯ _____

◯ _____

◯ _____

Healthy Habits Tracker

Year: _____

	Jan.	Feb.	Mar.	Apr.	May.	Jun.	Jul.	Aug.	Sep.	Oct.	Nov.	Dec.
1												
2												
3												
4												
5												
6												
7												
8												
9												
10												
11												
12												
13												
14												
15												
16												
17												
18												
19												
20												
21												
22												
23												
24												
25												
26												
27												
28												
29												
30												
31												

Mood:

◯ Happy

◯ Sad/Depressed

◯ Angry

◯ Anxious

◯ _____

◯ _____

◯ _____

◯ _____

Healthy Habits Tracker

Year: _____

	Jan.	Feb.	Mar.	Apr.	May.	Jun.	Jul.	Aug.	Sep.	Oct.	Nov.	Dec.
1												
2												
3												
4												
5												
6												
7												
8												
9												
10												
11												
12												
13												
14												
15												
16												
17												
18												
19												
20												
21												
22												
23												
24												
25												
26												
27												
28												
29												
30												
31												

Mood:

◯ Happy

◯ Sad/Depressed

◯ Angry

◯ Anxious

◯ _____

◯ _____

◯ _____

◯ _____

POSITIVE VIBES

Daily Self Sobriety Recovery Journal

Morning Gratitude:

Date: .... / .... / ....

M T W Th F Sa Su

Today's Thoughts:

Today's Affirmation:

What I'm Proud Of:

My Plans For Tomorrow:

Am I Sober Today?

◯ YES

◯ NO

Stay Sober

Notes: _____

● **My Mood Today:**

☆ ☆ ☆ ☆ ☆

Daily Self Sobriety Recovery Journal

Morning Gratitude:

Date: .... / .... / ....

M T W Th F Sa Su

Today's Affirmation:

Today's Thoughts:

What I'm Proud Of:

Am I Sober Today?

◯ YES

◯ NO

My Plans For Tomorrow:

Stay Sober

Notes: _____

● My Mood Today:

☆ ☆ ☆ ☆ ☆

Daily Self Sobriety Recovery Journal

POSITIVE VIBES

Morning Gratitude:

♡ _____
♡ _____
♡ _____
♡ _____
♡ _____

Date: _____ / _____ / _____

M T W Th F Sa Su

Today's Affirmation:

♡ _____
♡ _____
♡ _____
♡ _____
♡ _____

Today's Thoughts:

♡ _____
♡ _____
♡ _____
♡ _____
♡ _____

What I'm Proud Of:

♡ _____
♡ _____
♡ _____
♡ _____
♡ _____

Am I Sober Today?

◯ YES

◯ NO

My Plans For Tomorrow:

♡ _____
♡ _____
♡ _____
♡ _____
♡ _____

Stay Sober

Notes: _____

_____
_____
_____
_____
_____

● My Mood Today:

☆ ☆ ☆ ☆ ☆

....
....
....
....

Daily Self Sobriety Recovery Journal

POSITIVE VIBES

Morning Gratitude:

Date: _____ / _____ / _____

M T W Th F Sa Su

Today's Thoughts:

Today's Affirmation:

What I'm Proud Of:

My Plans For Tomorrow:

Am I Sober Today?

◯ YES

◯ NO

Stay Sober

Notes: _____

● **My Mood Today:**

☆ ☆ ☆ ☆ ☆

Daily Self Sobriety Recovery Journal

POSITIVE VIBES

Morning Gratitude:

Date: .... / .... / ....

M T W Th F Sa Su

Today's Thoughts:

Today's Affirmation:

What I'm Proud Of:

My Plans For Tomorrow:

Am I Sober Today?

◯ YES

◯ NO

Stay Sober

Notes: _____

● **My Mood Today:**

☆ ☆ ☆ ☆ ☆

Daily Self Sobriety Recovery Journal

POSITIVE VIBES

Morning Gratitude:

Date: .... / .... / ....
M T W Th F Sa Su

♡ --------------------------
♡ --------------------------
♡ --------------------------
♡ --------------------------
♡ --------------------------

Today's Thoughts:

♡ --------------------------
♡ --------------------------
♡ --------------------------
♡ --------------------------
♡ --------------------------

Today's Affirmation:

♡ --------------------------
♡ --------------------------
♡ --------------------------
♡ --------------------------
♡ --------------------------

What I'm Proud Of:

♡ --------------------------
♡ --------------------------
♡ --------------------------
♡ --------------------------
♡ --------------------------

My Plans For Tomorrow:

♡ --------------------------
♡ --------------------------
♡ --------------------------
♡ --------------------------
♡ --------------------------

Am I Sober Today?

◯ YES

♡ --------------------------
♡ --------------------------

◯ NO

♡ --------------------------
♡ --------------------------

Stay Sober

Notes: _____

_____
_____
_____
_____
_____

● My Mood Today:

☆ ☆ ☆ ☆ ☆

·····································
·····································
·····································
·····································
·····································

Daily Self Sobriety Recovery Journal

POSITIVE VIBES

Morning Gratitude:

- ♡ _____
- ♡ _____
- ♡ _____
- ♡ _____
- ♡ _____
- ♡ _____

Date: _____ / _____ / _____

M   T   W   Th   F   Sa   Su

Today's Affirmation:

- ♡ _____
- ♡ _____
- ♡ _____
- ♡ _____
- ♡ _____
- ♡ _____

Today's Thoughts:

- ♡ _____
- ♡ _____
- ♡ _____
- ♡ _____
- ♡ _____
- ♡ _____

What I'm Proud Of:

- ♡ _____
- ♡ _____
- ♡ _____
- ♡ _____
- ♡ _____
- ♡ _____

Am I Sober Today?

○ YES

○ NO

My Plans For Tomorrow:

- ♡ _____
- ♡ _____
- ♡ _____
- ♡ _____
- ♡ _____
- ♡ _____

Stay Sober

Notes: _____
_____
_____
_____
_____
_____
_____

● My Mood Today:

☆ ☆ ☆ ☆ ☆

....
....
....
....
....

Daily Self Sobriety Recovery Journal

POSITIVE VIBES

Morning Gratitude:

Date: _____ / _____ / _____

M T W Th F Sa Su

Today's Affirmation:

Today's Thoughts:

What I'm Proud Of:

Am I Sober Today?

◯ YES

◯ NO

My Plans For Tomorrow:

Stay Sober

Notes: _____

● **My Mood Today:**

☆ ☆ ☆ ☆ ☆

Daily Self Sobriety Recovery Journal

POSITIVE VIBES

Morning Gratitude:

Date: .... / .... / ....

M T W Th F Sa Su

Today's Thoughts:

Today's Affirmation:

What I'm Proud Of:

My Plans For Tomorrow:

Am I Sober Today?

◯ YES

◯ NO

Stay Sober

Notes: _____

● **My Mood Today:**

Daily Self Sobriety
Recovery Journal

POSITIVE VIBES

Morning Gratitude:

Date: .... / .... / ....
M T W Th F Sa Su

Today's Affirmation:

Today's Thoughts:

What I'm Proud Of:

Am I Sober Today?

◯ YES

◯ NO

My Plans For Tomorrow:

Stay Sober

Notes: _____

● **My Mood Today:**

☆ ☆ ☆ ☆ ☆

Daily Self Sobriety Recovery Journal

POSITIVE VIBES

Morning Gratitude:

Date: ___ / ___ / ___

M T W Th F Sa Su

Today's Thoughts:

Today's Affirmation:

What I'm Proud Of:

My Plans For Tomorrow:

Am I Sober Today?

○ YES

○ NO

Stay Sober

Notes: _____

_____

_____

_____

_____

_____

● My Mood Today:

☆ ☆ ☆ ☆ ☆

Daily Self Sobriety Recovery Journal

POSITIVE VIBES

Morning Gratitude:

- ♡ ....
- ♡ ....
- ♡ ....
- ♡ ....
- ♡ ....

Date: .... / .... / ....

M T W Th F Sa Su

Today's Affirmation:

- ♡ ....
- ♡ ....
- ♡ ....
- ♡ ....
- ♡ ....

Today's Thoughts:

- ♡ ....
- ♡ ....
- ♡ ....
- ♡ ....
- ♡ ....

What I'm Proud Of:

- ♡ ....
- ♡ ....
- ♡ ....
- ♡ ....
- ♡ ....

Am I Sober Today?

- ○ YES
- ♡ ....
- ○ NO
- ♡ ....

My Plans For Tomorrow:

- ♡ ....
- ♡ ....
- ♡ ....
- ♡ ....
- ♡ ....

Stay Sober

Notes: _____
_____
_____
_____
_____
_____
_____

● **My Mood Today:**

☆ ☆ ☆ ☆ ☆

....
....
....
....

Daily Self Sobriety Recovery Journal

POSITIVE VIBES

Morning Gratitude:

Date: ..../......../..........
M T W Th F Sa Su

Today's Affirmation:

Today's Thoughts:

What I'm Proud Of:

Am I Sober Today?

◯ YES

◯ NO

My Plans For Tomorrow:

Stay Sober

Notes: _____

● **My Mood Today:**

Daily Self Sobriety Recovery Journal

Morning Gratitude:

Date: .... / .... / ....

M T W Th F Sa Su

Today's Thoughts:

Today's Affirmation:

What I'm Proud Of:

My Plans For Tomorrow:

Am I Sober Today?

○ YES

○ NO

Stay Sober

Notes: _____

● **My Mood Today:**

Daily Self Sobriety Recovery Journal

POSITIVE VIBES

Morning Gratitude:

Date: ...... / ...... / ......

M T W Th F Sa Su

Today's Affirmation:

Today's Thoughts:

What I'm Proud Of:

Am I Sober Today?

○ YES

○ NO

My Plans For Tomorrow:

Stay Sober

Notes: _____

● **My Mood Today:**

☆ ☆ ☆ ☆ ☆

Daily Self Sobriety Recovery Journal

Morning Gratitude:

Date: .... / .... / ....

M T W Th F Sa Su

- ❤ ....
- ❤ ....
- ❤ ....
- ❤ ....
- ❤ ....

Today's Thoughts:

- ❤ ....
- ❤ ....
- ❤ ....
- ❤ ....
- ❤ ....

Today's Affirmation:

- ❤ ....
- ❤ ....
- ❤ ....
- ❤ ....
- ❤ ....

What I'm Proud Of:

- ❤ ....
- ❤ ....
- ❤ ....
- ❤ ....
- ❤ ....

Am I Sober Today?

○ YES

○ NO

My Plans For Tomorrow:

- ❤ ....
- ❤ ....
- ❤ ....
- ❤ ....
- ❤ ....

Stay Sober

Notes: ....

....

....

....

....

....

● My Mood Today:

☆ ☆ ☆ ☆ ☆

....

....

....

....

Daily Self Sobriety Recovery Journal

POSITIVE VIBES

Morning Gratitude:

Date: _____ / _____ / _____

M T W Th F Sa Su

Today's Affirmation:

Today's Thoughts:

What I'm Proud Of:

Am I Sober Today?

◯ YES

◯ NO

My Plans For Tomorrow:

Stay Sober

Notes: _____

● **My Mood Today:**

☆ ☆ ☆ ☆ ☆

Daily Self Sobriety Recovery Journal

POSITIVE VIBES

Morning Gratitude:

Date: .... / .... / ....
M T W Th F Sa Su

Today's Affirmation:

Today's Thoughts:

What I'm Proud Of:

Am I Sober Today?

◯ YES

◯ NO

My Plans For Tomorrow:

Stay Sober

Notes: _____

● **My Mood Today:**

☆ ☆ ☆ ☆ ☆

Daily Self Sobriety Recovery Journal

POSITIVE VIBES

Morning Gratitude:

Date: .... / .... / ....
M   T   W   Th   F   Sa   Su

Today's Thoughts:

Today's Affirmation:

What I'm Proud Of:

My Plans For Tomorrow:

Am I Sober Today?

◯ YES

◯ NO

Stay Sober

Notes: _____

● My Mood Today:

☆ ☆ ☆ ☆ ☆

Daily Self Sobriety Recovery Journal

POSITIVE VIBES

Morning Gratitude:

Date: _____ / _____ / _____
M T W Th F Sa Su

- ♡ -------------------------------
- ♡ -------------------------------
- ♡ -------------------------------
- ♡ -------------------------------
- ♡ -------------------------------

Today's Thoughts:

- ♡ -------------------------------
- ♡ -------------------------------
- ♡ -------------------------------
- ♡ -------------------------------
- ♡ -------------------------------

Today's Affirmation:

- ♡ -------------------------------
- ♡ -------------------------------
- ♡ -------------------------------
- ♡ -------------------------------
- ♡ -------------------------------
- ♡ -------------------------------

What I'm Proud Of:

- ♡ -------------------------------
- ♡ -------------------------------
- ♡ -------------------------------
- ♡ -------------------------------
- ♡ -------------------------------

My Plans For Tomorrow:

- ♡ -------------------------------
- ♡ -------------------------------
- ♡ -------------------------------
- ♡ -------------------------------
- ♡ -------------------------------

Am I Sober Today?

- ○ YES
- ♡ -------------------------------
- ♡ -------------------------------
- ○ NO
- ♡ -------------------------------
- ♡ -------------------------------

Stay Sober

Notes: _____

● **My Mood Today:**

☆ ☆ ☆ ☆ ☆

Daily Self Sobriety Recovery Journal

Morning Gratitude:

Date: .... / .... / ....

M T W Th F Sa Su

♡ _____
♡ _____
♡ _____
♡ _____
♡ _____

Today's Thoughts:

♡ _____
♡ _____
♡ _____
♡ _____
♡ _____

Today's Affirmation:

♡ _____
♡ _____
♡ _____
♡ _____
♡ _____

What I'm Proud Of:

♡ _____
♡ _____
♡ _____
♡ _____
♡ _____

Am I Sober Today?

◯ YES

♡ _____
♡ _____

◯ NO

♡ _____
♡ _____

My Plans For Tomorrow:

♡ _____
♡ _____
♡ _____
♡ _____
♡ _____

Stay Sober

Notes: _____
_____
_____
_____
_____
_____
_____

● My Mood Today:

☆ ☆ ☆ ☆ ☆

....
....
....
....
....

Daily Self Sobriety Recovery Journal

Morning Gratitude:

Date: .... / .... / ....

M   T   W   Th   F   Sa   Su

Today's Affirmation:

Today's Thoughts:

What I'm Proud Of:

Am I Sober Today?

○ YES

○ NO

My Plans For Tomorrow:

Stay Sober

Notes:

● My Mood Today:

☆ ☆ ☆ ☆ ☆

Daily Self Sobriety Recovery Journal

POSITIVE VIBES

Morning Gratitude:

Date: .... / .... / ....

M   T   W   Th   F   Sa   Su

Today's Affirmation:

Today's Thoughts:

What I'm Proud Of:

Am I Sober Today?

○ YES

○ NO

My Plans For Tomorrow:

Stay Sober

Notes: _____

● My Mood Today:

☆ ☆ ☆ ☆ ☆

Daily Self Sobriety Recovery Journal

POSITIVE VIBES

Morning Gratitude:

Date: ____ / ____ / ____
M T W Th F Sa Su

Today's Affirmation:

Today's Thoughts:

What I'm Proud Of:

Am I Sober Today?

○ YES

○ NO

My Plans For Tomorrow:

Stay Sober

Notes: _____

● **My Mood Today:**

☆ ☆ ☆ ☆ ☆

POSITIVE VIBES

Daily Self Sobriety Recovery Journal

Morning Gratitude:

Date: _____ / _____ / _____

M T W Th F Sa Su

Today's Thoughts:

Today's Affirmation:

What I'm Proud Of:

My Plans For Tomorrow:

Am I Sober Today?

◯ YES

◯ NO

Stay Sober

Notes: _____

● My Mood Today:

☆ ☆ ☆ ☆ ☆

Daily Self Sobriety Recovery Journal

POSITIVE VIBES

Morning Gratitude:

♡ ....
♡ ....
♡ ....
♡ ....
♡ ....
♡ ....

Date: .... / .... / ....

M T W Th F Sa Su

Today's Affirmation:

♡ ....
♡ ....
♡ ....
♡ ....
♡ ....
♡ ....

Today's Thoughts:

♡ ....
♡ ....
♡ ....
♡ ....
♡ ....
♡ ....

What I'm Proud Of:

♡ ....
♡ ....
♡ ....
♡ ....
♡ ....
♡ ....

Am I Sober Today?

◯ YES

♡ ....
♡ ....

◯ NO

♡ ....

My Plans For Tomorrow:

♡ ....
♡ ....
♡ ....
♡ ....
♡ ....
♡ ....

Stay Sober

Notes: _____

_____
_____
_____
_____
_____
_____

● My Mood Today:

☆ ☆ ☆ ☆ ☆

....
....
....
....
....

Daily Self Sobriety Recovery Journal

POSITIVE VIBES

Morning Gratitude:

♡ ....
♡ ....
♡ ....
♡ ....
♡ ....

Date: .... / .... / ....

M T W Th F Sa Su

Today's Affirmation:

♡ ....
♡ ....
♡ ....
♡ ....
♡ ....

Today's Thoughts:

♡ ....
♡ ....
♡ ....
♡ ....
♡ ....

What I'm Proud Of:

♡ ....
♡ ....
♡ ....
♡ ....

Am I Sober Today?

◯ YES

◯ NO

My Plans For Tomorrow:

♡ ....
♡ ....
♡ ....
♡ ....

Stay Sober

Notes: _____

_____
_____
_____
_____
_____

● My Mood Today:

☆ ☆ ☆ ☆ ☆

....
....
....
....
....

Daily Self Sobriety Recovery Journal

Morning Gratitude:

Date: _____ / _____ / _____

M T W Th F Sa Su

♡ ....
♡ ....
♡ ....
♡ ....
♡ ....

Today's Affirmation:

♡ ....
♡ ....
♡ ....
♡ ....
♡ ....

What I'm Proud Of:

♡ ....
♡ ....
♡ ....
♡ ....
♡ ....

Am I Sober Today?

◯ YES

♡ ....

◯ NO

♡ ....
♡ ....

Today's Thoughts:

♡ ....
♡ ....
♡ ....
♡ ....
♡ ....

My Plans For Tomorrow:

♡ ....
♡ ....
♡ ....
♡ ....
♡ ....

Stay Sober

Notes: _____

_____
_____
_____
_____
_____
_____

● My Mood Today:

☆ ☆ ☆ ☆ ☆

....
....
....
....

Daily Self Sobriety Recovery Journal

POSITIVE VIBES

Morning Gratitude:

Date: .... / .... / ....

M T W Th F Sa Su

Today's Thoughts:

Today's Affirmation:

What I'm Proud Of:

My Plans For Tomorrow:

Am I Sober Today?

◯ YES

◯ NO

Stay Sober

Notes: _____

● My Mood Today:

☆ ☆ ☆ ☆ ☆

Daily Self Sobriety Recovery Journal

POSITIVE VIBES

Morning Gratitude:

Date: ...... / ...... / ......

M T W Th F Sa Su

Today's Thoughts:

Today's Affirmation:

What I'm Proud Of:

My Plans For Tomorrow:

Am I Sober Today?

◯ YES

◯ NO

Stay Sober

Notes: _____

● **My Mood Today:**

Daily Self Sobriety Recovery Journal

POSITIVE VIBES

Morning Gratitude:

Date: .... / .... / ....

M T W Th F Sa Su

Today's Thoughts:

Today's Affirmation:

What I'm Proud Of:

My Plans For Tomorrow:

Am I Sober Today?

◯ YES

◯ NO

Stay Sober

Notes: _____

● My Mood Today:

☆ ☆ ☆ ☆ ☆

Daily Self Sobriety Recovery Journal

POSITIVE VIBES

Morning Gratitude:

Date: _____ / _____ / _____

M T W Th F Sa Su

- ♡ ....
- ♡ ....
- ♡ ....
- ♡ ....
- ♡ ....

Today's Affirmation:

- ♡ ....
- ♡ ....
- ♡ ....
- ♡ ....
- ♡ ....

Today's Thoughts:

- ♡ ....
- ♡ ....
- ♡ ....
- ♡ ....
- ♡ ....

What I'm Proud Of:

- ♡ ....
- ♡ ....
- ♡ ....
- ♡ ....
- ♡ ....

Am I Sober Today?

○ YES

- ♡ ....
- ♡ ....

○ NO

- ♡ ....
- ♡ ....

My Plans For Tomorrow:

- ♡ ....
- ♡ ....
- ♡ ....
- ♡ ....
- ♡ ....

Stay Sober

Notes: _____
_____
_____
_____
_____
_____
_____

● My Mood Today:

☆ ☆ ☆ ☆ ☆

....
....
....
....

POSITIVE VIBES

Daily Self Sobriety Recovery Journal

Morning Gratitude:

Date: _____ / _____ / _____

M T W Th F Sa Su

♡ _____
♡ _____
♡ _____
♡ _____
♡ _____

Today's Affirmation:

♡ _____
♡ _____
♡ _____
♡ _____
♡ _____

Today's Thoughts:

♡ _____
♡ _____
♡ _____
♡ _____
♡ _____

What I'm Proud Of:

♡ _____
♡ _____
♡ _____
♡ _____
♡ _____

Am I Sober Today?

○ YES

♡ _____

○ NO

♡ _____

My Plans For Tomorrow:

♡ _____
♡ _____
♡ _____
♡ _____
♡ _____

Stay Sober

Notes: _____

_____
_____
_____
_____
_____

● My Mood Today:

☆ ☆ ☆ ☆ ☆

....
....
....
....
....

Daily Self Sobriety Recovery Journal

Morning Gratitude:

Date: _____ / _____ / _____

M T W Th F Sa Su

♡ ....
♡ ....
♡ ....
♡ ....
♡ ....

Today's Thoughts:

♡ ....
♡ ....
♡ ....
♡ ....
♡ ....

Today's Affirmation:

♡ ....
♡ ....
♡ ....
♡ ....
♡ ....
♡ ....

What I'm Proud Of:

♡ ....
♡ ....
♡ ....
♡ ....
♡ ....
♡ ....

My Plans For Tomorrow:

♡ ....
♡ ....
♡ ....
♡ ....
♡ ....

Am I Sober Today?

○ YES

○ NO

Stay Sober

Notes: _____

_____
_____
_____
_____
_____

● My Mood Today:

☆ ☆ ☆ ☆ ☆

....
....
....
....

Daily Self Sobriety
Recovery Journal

POSITIVE VIBES

Morning Gratitude:

Date: .... / .... / ....
M   T   W   Th   F   Sa   Su

Today's Affirmation:

Today's Thoughts:

What I'm Proud Of:

Am I Sober Today?

○ YES

○ NO

My Plans For Tomorrow:

Stay Sober

Notes: _____

● **My Mood Today:**

☆ ☆ ☆ ☆ ☆

Daily Self Sobriety Recovery Journal

POSITIVE VIBES

Morning Gratitude:

Date: ...... / ...... / ....

M T W Th F Sa Su

Today's Affirmation:

Today's Thoughts:

What I'm Proud Of:

Am I Sober Today?

○ YES

○ NO

My Plans For Tomorrow:

Stay Sober

Notes: _____

● **My Mood Today:**

☆ ☆ ☆ ☆ ☆

Daily Self Sobriety Recovery Journal

POSITIVE VIBES

Morning Gratitude:

Date: _____ / _____ / _____

M T W Th F Sa Su

Today's Affirmation:

Today's Thoughts:

What I'm Proud Of:

Am I Sober Today?

○ YES

○ NO

My Plans For Tomorrow:

Stay Sober

Notes:

● My Mood Today:

Daily Self Sobriety Recovery Journal

Morning Gratitude:

Date: .... / .... / ....
M T W Th F Sa Su

Today's Thoughts:

Today's Affirmation:

What I'm Proud Of:

My Plans For Tomorrow:

Am I Sober Today?

○ YES

○ NO

Stay Sober

Notes: _____

● **My Mood Today:**

☆ ☆ ☆ ☆ ☆

Daily Self Sobriety Recovery Journal

POSITIVE VIBES

Morning Gratitude:

Date: ...... / ...... / ......

M T W Th F Sa Su

Today's Thoughts:

Today's Affirmation:

What I'm Proud Of:

My Plans For Tomorrow:

Am I Sober Today?

○ YES

○ NO

Stay Sober

Notes: _____

● My Mood Today:

☆ ☆ ☆ ☆ ☆

Daily Self Sobriety Recovery Journal

POSITIVE VIBES

Morning Gratitude:

Date: .... / .... / ....

M T W Th F Sa Su

Today's Affirmation:

Today's Thoughts:

What I'm Proud Of:

Am I Sober Today?

◯ YES

◯ NO

My Plans For Tomorrow:

Stay Sober

Notes: _____

● **My Mood Today:**

☆ ☆ ☆ ☆ ☆

Daily Self Sobriety Recovery Journal

POSITIVE VIBES

Morning Gratitude:

Date: .... / .... / ....

M T W Th F Sa Su

Today's Thoughts:

Today's Affirmation:

What I'm Proud Of:

My Plans For Tomorrow:

Am I Sober Today?

◯ YES

◯ NO

Stay Sober

Notes: _____

_____

_____

_____

_____

_____

● My Mood Today:

☆ ☆ ☆ ☆ ☆

Daily Self Sobriety
Recovery Journal

Morning Gratitude:

Date: _____ / _____ / _____
M T W Th F Sa Su

Today's Thoughts:

Today's Affirmation:

What I'm Proud Of:

My Plans For Tomorrow:

Am I Sober Today?

○ YES

○ NO

Stay Sober

Notes: _____

● **My Mood Today:**

☆ ☆ ☆ ☆ ☆

Daily Self Sobriety Recovery Journal

POSITIVE VIBES

Morning Gratitude:

Date: .... / .... / ....

M T W Th F Sa Su

Today's Thoughts:

Today's Affirmation:

What I'm Proud Of:

My Plans For Tomorrow:

Am I Sober Today?

◯ YES

◯ NO

Stay Sober

Notes: _____

_____

_____

_____

_____

_____

● My Mood Today:

Daily Self Sobriety Recovery Journal

Morning Gratitude:

Date: _____ / _____ / _____

M   T   W   Th   F   Sa   Su

Today's Affirmation:

Today's Thoughts:

What I'm Proud Of:

My Plans For Tomorrow:

Am I Sober Today?

◯ YES

◯ NO

Stay Sober

Notes: _____

● **My Mood Today:**

☆ ☆ ☆ ☆ ☆

Daily Self Sobriety Recovery Journal

POSITIVE VIBES

Morning Gratitude:

♡ _____
♡ _____
♡ _____
♡ _____
♡ _____

Date: _____ / _____ / _____

M T W Th F Sa Su

Today's Affirmation:

♡ _____
♡ _____
♡ _____
♡ _____
♡ _____

Today's Thoughts:

♡ _____
♡ _____
♡ _____
♡ _____
♡ _____

What I'm Proud Of:

♡ _____
♡ _____
♡ _____
♡ _____
♡ _____

Am I Sober Today?

○ YES

♡ _____

○ NO

♡ _____

My Plans For Tomorrow:

♡ _____
♡ _____
♡ _____
♡ _____
♡ _____

Stay Sober

Notes: _____
_____
_____
_____
_____
_____

● My Mood Today:

☆ ☆ ☆ ☆ ☆

....
....
....
....
....

Daily Self Sobriety Recovery Journal

POSITIVE VIBES

Morning Gratitude:
- ♡ ....
- ♡ ....
- ♡ ....
- ♡ ....
- ♡ ....

Date: .... / .... / ....

M T W Th F Sa Su

Today's Affirmation:
- ♡ ....
- ♡ ....
- ♡ ....
- ♡ ....
- ♡ ....
- ♡ ....

Today's Thoughts:
- ♡ ....
- ♡ ....
- ♡ ....
- ♡ ....
- ♡ ....

What I'm Proud Of:
- ♡ ....
- ♡ ....
- ♡ ....
- ♡ ....
- ♡ ....
- ♡ ....

Am I Sober Today?

○ YES
- ♡ ....
- ♡ ....
○ NO
- ♡ ....
- ♡ ....

My Plans For Tomorrow:
- ♡ ....
- ♡ ....
- ♡ ....
- ♡ ....
- ♡ ....

Stay Sober

Notes: _____
_____
_____
_____
_____
_____

● My Mood Today:

☆ ☆ ☆ ☆ ☆

....
....
....
....
....

Daily Self Sobriety Recovery Journal

POSITIVE VIBES

Morning Gratitude:

Date: _____ / _____ / _____

M T W Th F Sa Su

Today's Affirmation:

Today's Thoughts:

What I'm Proud Of:

Am I Sober Today?

○ YES

○ NO

My Plans For Tomorrow:

Stay Sober

Notes: _____

● **My Mood Today:**

Daily Self Sobriety Recovery Journal

Morning Gratitude:

♡ _____
♡ _____
♡ _____
♡ _____

Date: _____ / _____ / _____

M T W Th F Sa Su

Today's Affirmation:

♡ _____
♡ _____
♡ _____
♡ _____
♡ _____
♡ _____

Today's Thoughts:

♡ _____
♡ _____
♡ _____
♡ _____
♡ _____

What I'm Proud Of:

♡ _____
♡ _____
♡ _____
♡ _____
♡ _____

Am I Sober Today?

◯ YES

♡ _____
♡ _____

◯ NO

♡ _____
♡ _____

My Plans For Tomorrow:

♡ _____
♡ _____
♡ _____
♡ _____
♡ _____

Stay Sober

Notes: _____
_____
_____
_____
_____
_____

● My Mood Today:

☆ ☆ ☆ ☆ ☆

_____
_____
_____
_____
_____

Daily Self Sobriety Recovery Journal

POSITIVE VIBES

Morning Gratitude:

Date: _____ / _____ / _____

M T W Th F Sa Su

♡ _____
♡ _____
♡ _____
♡ _____
♡ _____

Today's Affirmation:

♡ _____
♡ _____
♡ _____
♡ _____
♡ _____

Today's Thoughts:

♡ _____
♡ _____
♡ _____
♡ _____
♡ _____

What I'm Proud Of:

♡ _____
♡ _____
♡ _____
♡ _____
♡ _____

Am I Sober Today?

○ YES

♡ _____
♡ _____

○ NO

♡ _____
♡ _____

My Plans For Tomorrow:

♡ _____
♡ _____
♡ _____
♡ _____
♡ _____

Stay Sober

Notes: _____
_____
_____
_____
_____
_____
_____

● My Mood Today:

☆ ☆ ☆ ☆ ☆

....
....
....
....
....

Daily Self Sobriety
Recovery Journal

POSITIVE VIBES

Morning Gratitude:

♡ ....
♡ ....
♡ ....
♡ ....
♡ ....

Date: .... / .... / ....

M T W Th F Sa Su

Today's Affirmation:

♡ ....
♡ ....
♡ ....
♡ ....
♡ ....
♡ ....

Today's Thoughts:

♡ ....
♡ ....
♡ ....
♡ ....

What I'm Proud Of:

♡ ....
♡ ....
♡ ....
♡ ....

Am I Sober Today?

○ YES

♡ ....
♡ ....

○ NO

♡ ....
♡ ....

My Plans For Tomorrow:

♡ ....
♡ ....
♡ ....
♡ ....

Stay Sober

Notes: _____
_____
_____
_____
_____
_____

● My Mood Today:

☆ ☆ ☆ ☆ ☆

....
....
....
....

POSITIVE VIBES

Daily Self Sobriety Recovery Journal

Morning Gratitude:

Date: .... / .... / ....

M T W Th F Sa Su

Today's Thoughts:

Today's Affirmation:

What I'm Proud Of:

My Plans For Tomorrow:

Am I Sober Today?

◯ YES

◯ NO

Stay Sober

Notes: _____

● **My Mood Today:**

☆ ☆ ☆ ☆ ☆

Daily Self Sobriety Recovery Journal

POSITIVE VIBES

Morning Gratitude:

Date: _____ / _____ / _____

M   T   W   Th   F   Sa   Su

Today's Affirmation:

Today's Thoughts:

What I'm Proud Of:

Am I Sober Today?

○ YES

○ NO

My Plans For Tomorrow:

Stay Sober

Notes: _____

● **My Mood Today:**

☆ ☆ ☆ ☆ ☆

Daily Self Sobriety Recovery Journal

POSITIVE VIBES

Morning Gratitude:

- ♡ ....
- ♡ ....
- ♡ ....
- ♡ ....
- ♡ ....

Date: .... / .... / ....

M T W Th F Sa Su

Today's Affirmation:

- ♡ ....
- ♡ ....
- ♡ ....
- ♡ ....
- ♡ ....

Today's Thoughts:

- ♡ ....
- ♡ ....
- ♡ ....
- ♡ ....
- ♡ ....

What I'm Proud Of:

- ♡ ....
- ♡ ....
- ♡ ....
- ♡ ....
- ♡ ....

Am I Sober Today?

◯ YES

- ♡ ....
- ♡ ....

◯ NO

- ♡ ....
- ♡ ....

My Plans For Tomorrow:

- ♡ ....
- ♡ ....
- ♡ ....
- ♡ ....
- ♡ ....

Stay Sober

Notes: _____

_____
_____
_____
_____
_____

● My Mood Today:

☆ ☆ ☆ ☆ ☆

....
....
....
....

Daily Self Sobriety Recovery Journal

POSITIVE VIBES

Morning Gratitude:
- ♡ ....
- ♡ ....
- ♡ ....
- ♡ ....
- ♡ ....

Date: ..../ ..../ ....
M T W Th F Sa Su

Today's Affirmation:
- ♡ ....
- ♡ ....
- ♡ ....
- ♡ ....
- ♡ ....

Today's Thoughts:
- ♡ ....
- ♡ ....
- ♡ ....
- ♡ ....
- ♡ ....

What I'm Proud Of:
- ♡ ....
- ♡ ....
- ♡ ....
- ♡ ....
- ♡ ....

Am I Sober Today?
○ YES

- ♡ ....
- ♡ ....

○ NO

- ♡ ....
- ♡ ....

My Plans For Tomorrow:
- ♡ ....
- ♡ ....
- ♡ ....
- ♡ ....
- ♡ ....

Stay Sober

Notes: ....
....
....
....
....
....
....

● My Mood Today:
☆ ☆ ☆ ☆ ☆
....
....
....
....
....

Daily Self Sobriety Recovery Journal

POSITIVE VIBES

Morning Gratitude:

Date: .... / .... / ....
M T W Th F Sa Su

Today's Thoughts:

Today's Affirmation:

What I'm Proud Of:

My Plans For Tomorrow:

Am I Sober Today?

◯ YES

◯ NO

Stay Sober

Notes: _____

● My Mood Today:

☆ ☆ ☆ ☆ ☆

Daily Self Sobriety Recovery Journal

POSITIVE VIBES

Morning Gratitude:

Date: _____ / _____ / _____

M T W Th F Sa Su

Today's Thoughts:

Today's Affirmation:

What I'm Proud Of:

My Plans For Tomorrow:

Am I Sober Today?

○ YES

○ NO

Stay Sober

Notes: _____

● **My Mood Today:**

☆ ☆ ☆ ☆ ☆

Daily Self Sobriety Recovery Journal

POSITIVE VIBES

Morning Gratitude:

Date: .... / .... / ....

M T W Th F Sa Su

♡ ....
♡ ....
♡ ....
♡ ....
♡ ....

Today's Affirmation:

♡ ....
♡ ....
♡ ....
♡ ....
♡ ....

Today's Thoughts:

♡ ....
♡ ....
♡ ....
♡ ....
♡ ....

What I'm Proud Of:

♡ ....
♡ ....
♡ ....
♡ ....
♡ ....

Am I Sober Today?

◯ YES

♡ ....
♡ ....

◯ NO

♡ ....
♡ ....

My Plans For Tomorrow:

♡ ....
♡ ....
♡ ....
♡ ....
♡ ....

Stay Sober

Notes: _____
_____
_____
_____
_____
_____

● My Mood Today:

☆ ☆ ☆ ☆ ☆

....
....
....
....
....

Daily Self Sobriety Recovery Journal

POSITIVE VIBES

Morning Gratitude:

Date: .... / .... / ....
M   T   W   Th   F   Sa   Su

♡ _____
♡ _____
♡ _____
♡ _____
♡ _____

Today's Thoughts:

♡ _____
♡ _____
♡ _____
♡ _____
♡ _____

Today's Affirmation:

♡ _____
♡ _____
♡ _____
♡ _____
♡ _____
♡ _____

What I'm Proud Of:

♡ _____
♡ _____
♡ _____
♡ _____
♡ _____

Am I Sober Today?

○ YES

○ NO

♡ _____
♡ _____
♡ _____

My Plans For Tomorrow:

♡ _____
♡ _____
♡ _____
♡ _____
♡ _____

Stay Sober

Notes: _____
_____
_____
_____
_____
_____

● My Mood Today:

☆ ☆ ☆ ☆ ☆

....
....
....
....

Daily Self Sobriety Recovery Journal

POSITIVE VIBES

Morning Gratitude:

Date: .... / .... / ....

M T W Th F Sa Su

♡ ....
♡ ....
♡ ....
♡ ....
♡ ....

Today's Affirmation:

♡ ....
♡ ....
♡ ....
♡ ....
♡ ....
♡ ....

Today's Thoughts:

♡ ....
♡ ....
♡ ....
♡ ....
♡ ....
♡ ....

What I'm Proud Of:

♡ ....
♡ ....
♡ ....
♡ ....
♡ ....

Am I Sober Today?

○ YES

♡ ....
♡ ....

○ NO

♡ ....
♡ ....

My Plans For Tomorrow:

♡ ....
♡ ....
♡ ....
♡ ....
♡ ....

Stay Sober

Notes: _____
_____
_____
_____
_____
_____

● My Mood Today:

☆ ☆ ☆ ☆ ☆

....
....
....
....
....

Daily Self Sobriety
Recovery Journal

POSITIVE VIBES

Morning Gratitude:

♡ ....
♡ ....
♡ ....
♡ ....
♡ ....

Date: .... / .... / ....

M T W Th F Sa Su

Today's Affirmation:

♡ ....
♡ ....
♡ ....
♡ ....
♡ ....

Today's Thoughts:

♡ ....
♡ ....
♡ ....
♡ ....
♡ ....

What I'm Proud Of:

♡ ....
♡ ....
♡ ....
♡ ....
♡ ....

Am I Sober Today?

○ YES

♡ ....
♡ ....

○ NO

♡ ....

My Plans For Tomorrow:

♡ ....
♡ ....
♡ ....
♡ ....
♡ ....

Stay Sober

Notes: _____
_____
_____
_____
_____
_____

● My Mood Today:

☆ ☆ ☆ ☆ ☆

....
....
....
....
....

Reflect and Journal
on the lines below

Reflect and Journal
on the lines below

Reflect and Journal
on the lines below

Reflect and Journal
on the lines below

Reflect and Journal
on the lines below

_____

_____

_____

_____

_____

_____

_____

_____

_____

_____

_____

_____

_____

Reflect and Journal
on the lines below

_____

_____

_____

_____

_____

_____

_____

_____

_____

_____

_____

_____

_____

_____

Reflect and Journal
on the lines below

Reflect and Journal
on the lines below

Reflect and Journal
on the lines below

Reflect and Journal
on the lines below

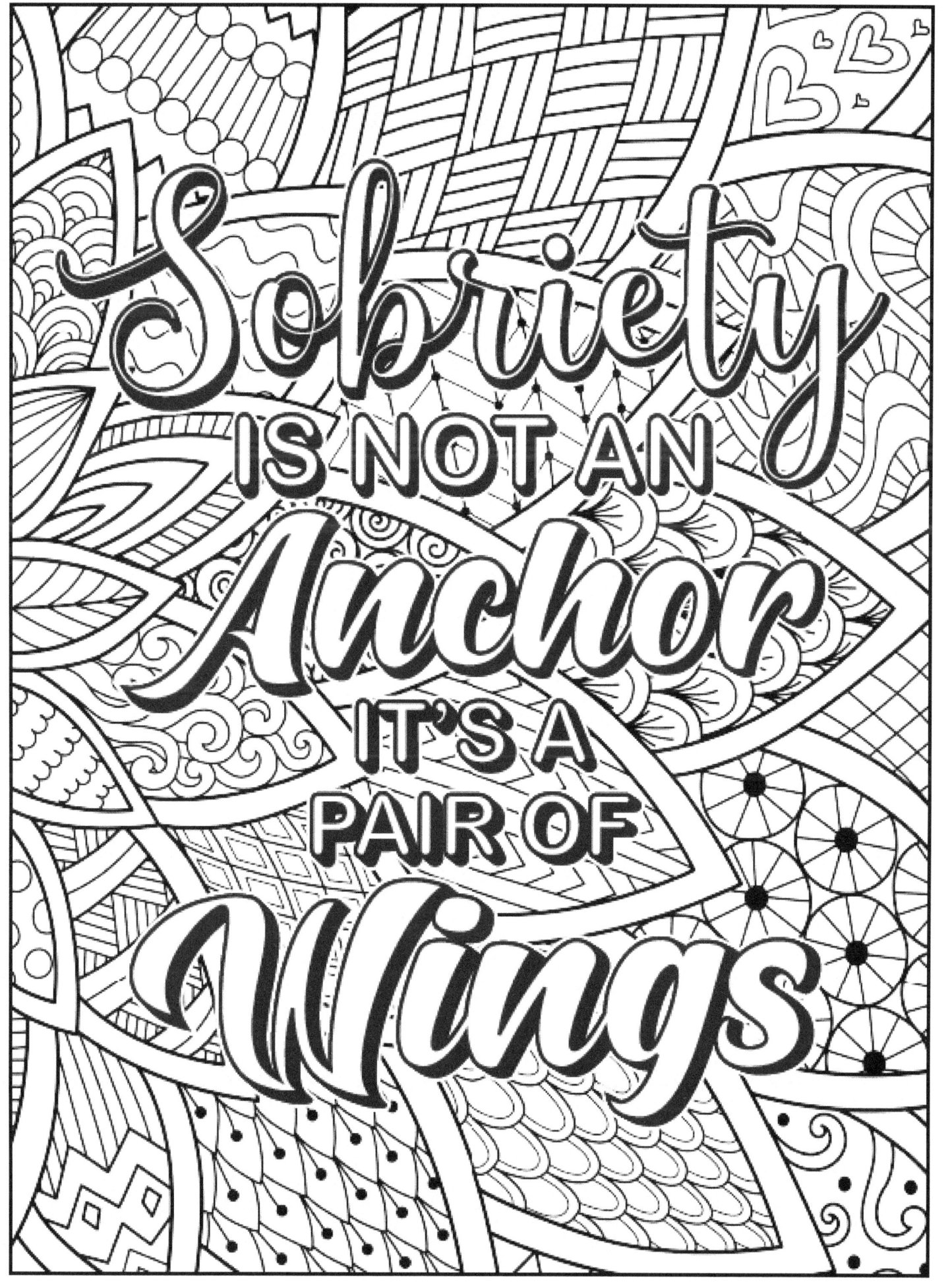

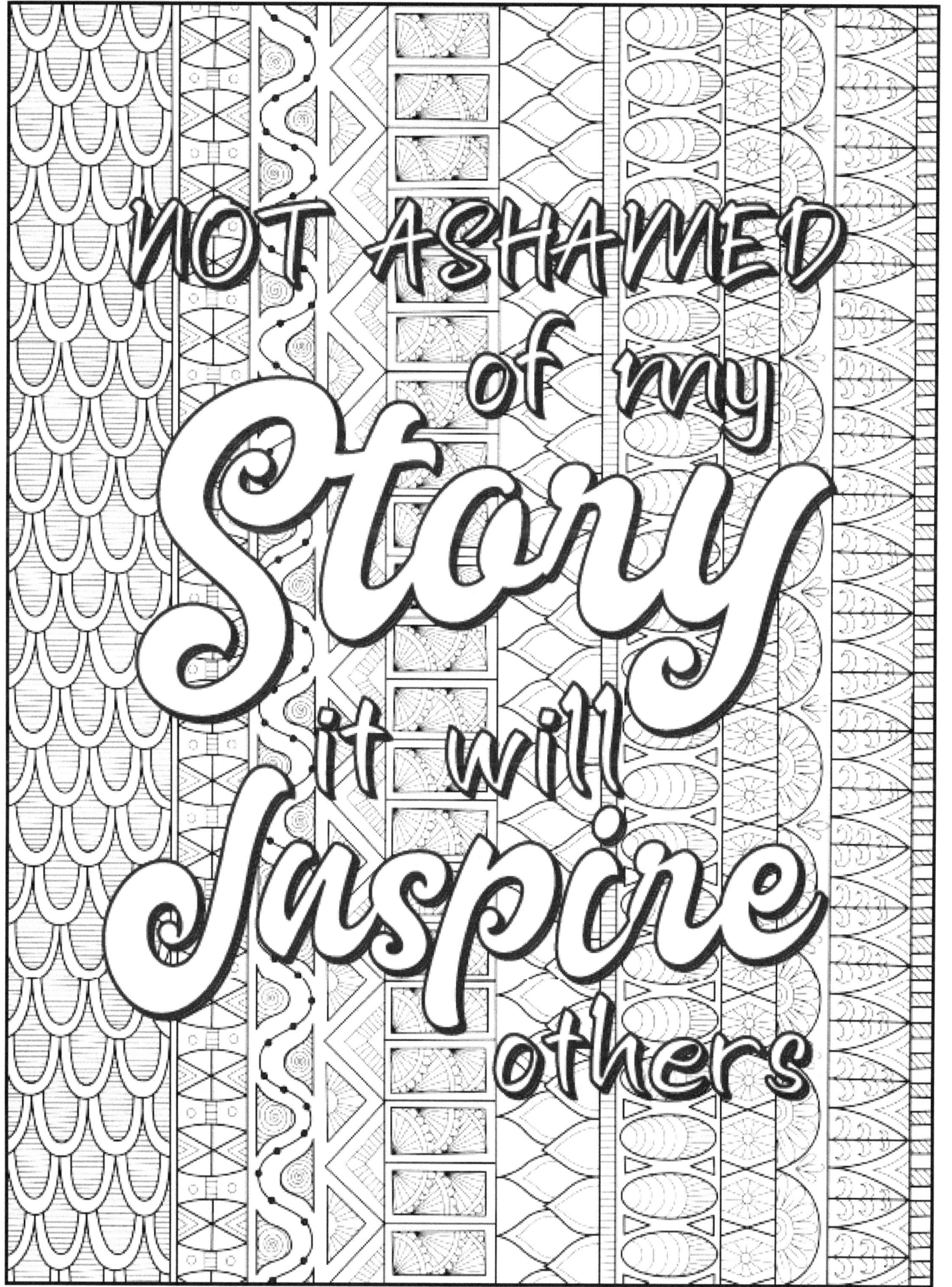

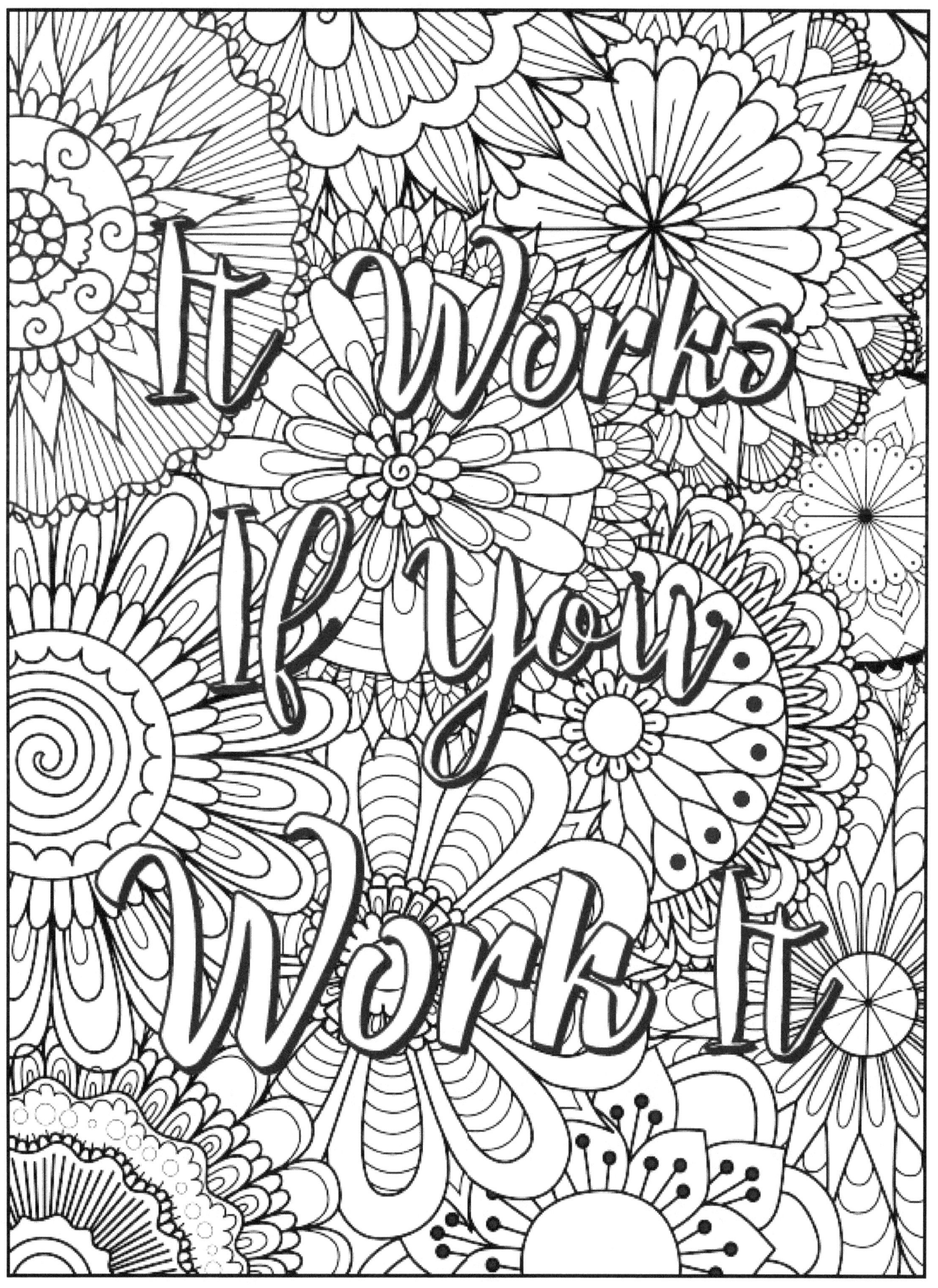

Printed in the USA
CPSIA information can be obtained
at www.ICGtesting.com
CBHW061937121223
2596CB00011B/117